D0579413

CHOOSING NEWS

WHAT GETS REPORTED AND WHY

by Barb Palser

Content Consultant: John V. Pavlik,
Professor and Chair, Department of Journalism and Media Studies,
School of Communication and Information, Rutgers University

COMPASS POINT BOOKS
a capstone imprint

CONCORDIA UNIVERSITY LIBRARY
PORTLAND OR 97211

EXPLORING
MEDIA LITERACY

Compass Point Books
1710 Roe Crest Drive
North Mankato, MN 56003

Copyright © 2012 by Compass Point Books, a Capstone imprint.
All rights reserved. No part of this book may be reproduced without written
permission from the publisher. The publisher takes no responsibility for the use of
any of the materials or methods described in this book, nor for the products thereof.

Editor: Mari Kesselring
Designers: Becky Daum and Christa Schneider

Image Credits
Herbert Kratky/Shutterstock Images, cover (top); Shutterstock Images, cover
(middle), 7, 16, 36, 62; Ric Feld/AP Images, cover (bottom); Davide Illini/
iStockphoto, back cover (left); Florian ISPAS/Shutterstock Images, back cover
(center); M. Dykstra/Shutterstock Images, back cover (right); iStockphoto, 5, 10,
68; Red Line Editorial, 6, 18, 37, 42; Kyodo News/AP Images, 9; Mark J. Terrill/
AP Images, 11; Henryk Sadura/iStockphoto, 13; Daniel Stein/iStockphoto, 14;
Christopher Halloran/Shutterstock Images, 19; Troels Graugaard/iStockphoto, 21;
Evan Vucci/AP Images, 22; Bonnie Jacobs/iStockphoto, 27, 65; Lennart Preiss/
AP Images, 28; Lynne Sladky/AP Images, 31; Rex Features/AP Images, 33; Zmeel
Photography/iStockphoto, 35; Kathy Willens/AP Images, 38; H. Rumph Jr/AP
Images, 44; Nancy Ross/iStockphoto, 49; Prashant Zi/Fotolia, 50; Mike Mergen/AP
Images, 55; Robyn Beck/AFP/Getty Images, 57; Manuel Velasco/iStockphoto, 61;
Artur Marciniec/iStockphoto, 67; Jianhao Guan/Shutterstock Images, 71; Muharrem
Öner/iStockphoto, 75

Design elements: Becky Daum/Red Line Editorial

This book was manufactured with paper containing at least
10 percent post-consumer waste.

Library of Congress Cataloging-in-Publication Data
Palser, Barb.
 Choosing news : what gets reported and why / by Barb Palser.
    p. cm.—(Media literacy)
Includes bibliographical references and index.
ISBN 978-0-7565-4517-8 (library binding)
ISBN 978-0-7565-4537-6 (paperback)
1. Journalism—Juvenile literature. 2. Reporters and
reporting—Juvenile literature. I. Title. II. Series.
PN4731.P245 2012
070.4—dc23   2011025697

Visit Compass Point Books on the Internet at *www.capstonepub.com*

Printed in the United States of America in Stevens Point, Wisconsin.
102011   006404WZS12

CONTENTS

CHAPTER 1

WHAT IS NEWS?

"Call it the Awareness Instinct. We need news to live our lives, to protect ourselves, bond with each other, identify friends and enemies."

—*Bill Kovach and Tom Rosenstiel,*
The Elements of Journalism

How often do you watch the news on TV or read a newspaper? How often do you check news online?

Maybe you only see or hear news once in a while, when a family member is watching news in the same room or listening to news on the car radio. Maybe you accidentally find news when you are surfing the Internet. Even if you're not interested in news right now, you probably will be someday.

More than 80 percent of adults read, watch, or listen to some news every day. They pay attention to news because it affects their lives. For example, if the government decides to raise taxes, people

would learn about it on the news. If scientists find a cure for a disease, people would find out about it on the news.

People also pay attention to the news because they want to know what's happening in the world. They want to know about wars, earthquakes, or other disasters that happen in other places.

The TV, newspaper, radio, magazine, and Internet companies that report the news are known as the news media or the media. When choosing which media sources to follow, it helps to know how the media work. How do reporters pick which news to report and which to ignore? What rules do reporters follow to avoid making mistakes? What is a media bias? And how do citizens help the media with news reporting?

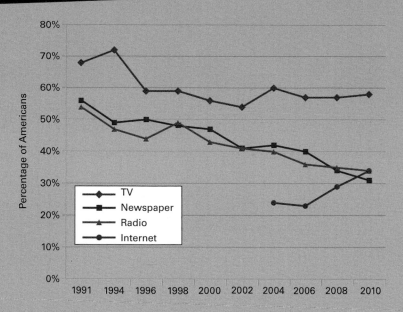

A 2010 poll that measured where Americans got their news on a given day had bad news for newspapers. For the first time more Americans got news from the Internet than from printed newspapers.

Television remained the main source of news while radio and print declined. Internet news sources include the websites of traditional print newspapers and TV and radio stations.

Source: Pew Research Center for the People and the Press

By learning the answers to these questions, you will discover the difference between actual news and information that is untrue. The more you know about how news companies make decisions, the more efficiently you can choose your news sources.

Defining News

News is simply a current event that is important to a group of people. That event could be a car

News is important to many people. Large screens in New York City's Times Square show news programs and breaking news updates. In the 21st century, there are many ways to receive news.

News is simply a current event that is important to a group of people.

accident, a political election, the discovery of dinosaur fossils, or even a movie star winning an award. All of these events can be news if they matter to people. But how do reporters determine what really is news? Here are some questions a reporter might ask to decide whether an event is news or not:

Did It Happen Recently?

In order to be news, an event must have happened recently or have been recently discovered. For example, a tornado that damaged a town yesterday would be news. But a tornado that happened two years ago would not be news. If the public has known about something for a while, then it is no longer news.

Something that happened in the past, but was recently revealed could also be news. For example, a government official committed a crime five years ago. But the crime has just been discovered. This is news because the public is learning about it for the first time.

The Japan earthquake and tsunami was top news when it occurred in March 2011 because it had just happened. The news media followed the story into May as Japan dealt with a resulting crisis at the Fukushima Nuclear Power Plant. But as time passed, most news companies stopped or decreased their reporting on the event. · · · · · · · · · · · · · · · · ·

Who Is the Audience of the Information?

Whether something is news also depends on the audience a reporter reaches. If a reporter works for a science magazine, the discovery of a new dinosaur fossil would probably be interesting to the magazine's readers. However, the same readers might not care about a movie star winning an award. For a science magazine, the definition of news would be limited to information about science.

Many reporters work for mass media—newspapers, TV stations, radio stations, magazines, and websites that reach many people. Big TV networks such as ABC, CBS, NBC, and CNN are examples of mass media. So are newspapers such as *The New York Times* and the *Los Angeles Times*. Local daily newspaper and TV stations are also mass media. Since mass media companies have a broad audience, they cover a range of topics. The four examples used earlier (a car accident, a political election, the discovery of dinosaur fossils, a movie star winning an award) all fit the definition of news for a mass media audience. Mass media are also called mainstream media because they appeal to the general public.

Since mass media companies have a broad audience, they cover a range of topics.

In 2011 many news companies reported on *Glee's* Golden Globe win for best comedy or musical television series. Mass media companies often cover some news about pop culture celebrities.

Does It Affect Many People?

A car accident that causes minor damage is not news, since many people are not affected. However, people living in the area would be affected if the accident causes a large traffic jam. If a woman was killed in the accident, it would be even bigger news because people would feel sorry for the woman. They would want to know details of the accident.

Even if it doesn't impact their lives, people are affected by news that stirs their emotions. Much of the news that is reported makes people feel emotions such as joy, sorrow, anger, or amusement—even if the news is happening to others. It's part of human nature to care about what happens to others.

Is It Controversial?

News stories that involve people or groups discussing laws, religion, the environment, or any other controversial topic also receive a great deal of attention.

Politics is a good example. It involves debate and affects many people. The media spend a lot of time covering politics, elections, and public policy. The public pays attention to politics because politicians affect the way we live our lives. Politicians help set the amount of taxes we pay and influence health policies and numerous other laws.

News stories that involve people or groups arguing over laws, religion, the environment, or any other controversial topic also receive a great deal of attention.

Is a Famous Person Involved?

Many stories become news only because a famous person is involved. If an average citizen is caught shoplifting, it would not make the news. However, if the shoplifter is a movie star, people want to know about it.

Is It Strange or Amazing?

A number of events are news simply because they are out of the ordinary. A woman who lived to be 114 years old, a female dog that adopted tiger cubs, and a skydiver who survived a 2-mile (3.2-kilometer) fall are news stories that attracted attention just because they were unusual.

There are many different types of news. Usually a single TV station or newspaper cannot possibly report all the news happening in an area. Reporters and news managers must pick the news that will be most interesting to their audience.

Making Decisions about the News

Pretend you are the editor of your city's newspaper. One of the editor's jobs is to decide

The *Chicago Tribune*'s offices are located on Michigan Avenue in Chicago, Illinois. Big news outlets have several offices around the world.

which stories to cover each day. The editor also chooses which story should be the lead story— the most important story on the front page of a newspaper or website. On TV or the radio, the lead story is the first story presented in the newscast. The lead story is sometimes called the top story because it appears at the top of a page or newscast.

Today you must pick which of these three stories should be the lead story:

Story #1: A mudslide has damaged a major road in your town. As a result the road will be closed for at least a week.

Story #2: A small airplane has crashed in another state, killing five people.

Story #3: A famous rock star has been arrested for drunk driving.

Which one of these stories would you pick as the lead story? In order to decide, the editor might use some of the questions posed earlier. Which story is most important to the audience of your local newspaper?

Most editors would select Story #1. It is important for people to know about the road closure, since many people drive on that road. People will need to be informed of detours. They will want to know when the road will re-open.

The plane crash is also big news. However, it does not affect the readers as much as the road closure. But if you are the editor of a national newspaper, your choice most likely would be the plane crash story. People around the country would be more concerned about a plane crash than a road closure in one town. The rock star arrested for drunk driving would also be interesting to people. However, it is less important than the other two stories.

People who work in mass media make decisions like this every day. They decide which stories will be most valuable to the people who receive the news.

Hard News and Entertainment News

News managers also decide how much hard news to provide and how much entertainment news to provide.

Hard news is news about important events that affect people's lives. A road closure and a plane crash are both examples of hard news. Wars, natural disasters, scientific discoveries, and political elections are also examples of hard news.

Entertainment news is news about celebrities, TV shows, movies, and music. Although entertainment news does not really affect a person's life, it is interesting to follow. A rock star being arrested for drunk driving is entertainment news. News that combines information with entertainment is sometimes called "infotainment."

Some journalists believe that entertainment news is a waste of time. They feel it is the media's responsibility to inform the public about important events, not to entertain people with celebrity gossip. Some news companies decide to cover little or no entertainment news at all.

At times entertainment news attracts larger audiences than hard news. Larger audiences help news companies earn more money. For this reason many newspapers and TV newscasts present a mix of hard news and entertainment news.

What Does the Public Want?

Mainstream news companies tend to focus on stories that attract the attention of the general public. Typically the mainstream media are successful when choosing which stories will be most appealing to the public. Occasionally they fall off the track and pick the wrong story.

Mainstream news companies tend to focus on stories that attract the attention of the general public.

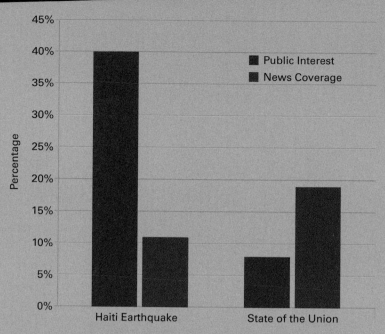

Public Interest
News Coverage

Percentage

45%
40%
35%
30%
25%
20%
15%
10%
5%
0%

Haiti Earthquake   State of the Union

In the last week of January 2010, the media spent more time covering President Obama's State of the Union address than the aftermath of the Haiti earthquake. However, the general public was much more interested in the Haiti earthquake.

Source: Pew Research Center for the People and the Press

For example, in the days following the 2010 Haiti earthquake, the national news media spent more time covering that story than any other story.

At the time most Americans agreed that the Haiti earthquake was the most important news. After a few weeks, the media moved on to cover other stories. Only 8 percent of news coverage was given to the Haiti earthquake. Yet 40 percent of Americans said they were still following the Haiti story more closely than any other story.

Other times the media may spend too much time covering a story. This often happens with political speeches. For example, when President Barack Obama gave his State of the Union address in January 2010, the national media covered the story for several days, even after the general public lost interest.

What do you think? Should news managers report stories based on what they think is most important—or what attracts the public? What would happen if the media only covered stories that were popular with the general public?

CHAPTER 2

ACCURACY AND CREDIBILITY

"Credibility is a journalist's most important asset, and accuracy is the best way to protect it."

— *Debora Halpern Wenger,* Advancing the Story: Broadcast Journalism in a Multimedia World

Reporters have an important role in a free society. Without reporters to inform the public, people would not have the information they need to vote for lawmakers who will protect their interests. The public may not know about crime in their neighborhoods, political corruption, unsafe products, or pollution in the environment.

Because a reporter's job is so important, you may expect there would be rules about what reporters can and cannot do, or who can be a reporter. For example, doctors and lawyers are required to go to college and pass tests

before the government allows them to practice medicine or law.

There are very few laws in the United States that limit reporters. This is largely due to the First Amendment to the United States Constitution. The First Amendment says: "Congress shall make no law respecting an establishment of religion, or prohibiting the free exercise thereof; or abridging the freedom of speech, or of the press; or the right of the people peaceably to assemble, and to petition the Government for a redress of grievances."

The part of the First Amendment that deals with the media says that Congress cannot make laws that restrict the freedom of the press. That means that the government cannot control what reporters write or say. The government cannot pick who can be a reporter either. Preventing the media from publishing information is known as censorship.

Student reporters who work for news outlets run by their schools and universities are sometimes censored. Many students protest against this type of censorship. ·

Freedom of the Press

Freedom of the press is one of the most basic requirements of a truly free and democratic society. If the government controlled the press, then politicians could easily censor the media from exposing corruption or incompetence. The government could go against citizens' constitutional rights without anyone knowing. The government could even force the media to report biased information that shows corrupt officials or bad policies in a positive light. A country's greatest defense is a free press to keep its citizens aware of news without fear of censorship or penalty from the government.

Defamation

But the First Amendment doesn't mean that media can publish information that isn't true. Defamation is the sharing of false information that damages someone's reputation. A false statement is called libel when written in a newspaper. When a false statement is spoken on TV or radio, it's called slander. Both libel and slander are types of defamation.

Anyone can be sued for defamation, including news companies. But the subject of the false statement must prove the news company was careless. That means the news company was not careful to find out whether the information was true. If the untrue statement is about a public figure, he or she must prove that the news company published the false

A false statement is called libel when written in a newspaper. When a false statement is spoken on TV or radio, it's called slander.

information on purpose, in order to damage the person's reputation.

Defamation rules protect news companies and others from being sued for honest mistakes. If a news company was trying to report the truth but accidentally published false information, it would probably not be guilty of defamation.

Journalism Standards and Credibility

Although there are no laws that explain the rights of reporters, the media set their own rules

MEDIA CONTROL IN OTHER COUNTRIES

Many countries do not allow press freedom. In North Korea the government has complete control over the media. The North Korean government decides what information the public receives. It uses the media to glorify the country's leaders. It's common for the government to restrict Internet access too. This is to prevent the public from organizing against the government or accessing news from other countries. North Korea is not the only country with these rules. Eritrea, Turkmenistan, Cuba, Burma, and China are all countries that place limitations on the press.

about how reporters should do their jobs. In fact, there is a list of reporting rules that news companies have developed over time. These rules are often called standards.

News companies choose to follow journalistic standards in order to keep their credibility. Credibility is the public trust in a news company to report the news accurately and fairly. If people lose their trust in a news source, they will probably stop using it. They will find another source for their news.

Here are a few standards that news companies follow to protect their credibility:

Accuracy and Verification

The basic responsibility of a reporter is to get the facts right. Journalistic standards say that reporters should verify all information they publish. Verification means confirming facts by witnessing them directly. If a reporter did not witness a news event, the reporter should find at least two reliable sources who did.

Identifying Sources

When reporters use eyewitnesses and experts to help report a story, they need to identify those witnesses and experts. They should give credit to the witness and report the person's connection to the story.

One exception to this rule is anonymous sources. Anonymous sources are people who do not want to be named in a news story. Sources may remain anonymous to protect themselves. For example, if a woman talked to a reporter about unsafe conditions at the factory where she worked, she might not want her name in the story because she could get fired. Reporters try to avoid using anonymous sources in news stories unless that's the only way to get information.

Looking at All Sides

When a story involves conflict between two or more people or groups, journalistic standards say that a reporter should try to speak with people on all sides of the conflict. For example, if a factory is accused of unsafe working conditions, the reporter should listen to the employees' side of the story. But the reporter should also ask the factory owner for his or her side of the story. If the factory owner refuses to talk, then the reporter can explain that the factory owner declined to comment.

A reporter often interviews people in order to get the facts of a story or the public's response to an event. There are very few laws about what a reporter can report. However, reporters follow a list of rules called journalistic standards. . . . .

Respect for Privacy

Occasionally reporters and news managers have to decide whether publishing certain information or showing certain images is worth the grief it may cause. For example, a newspaper may choose not to publish a photograph of a man who has discovered

Julian Assange is the founder of WikiLeaks, a website where people can submit classified documents or information for publication on the site anonymously. WikiLeaks's controversial releases of top-secret government information have led some to question the website's validity as a news source. ·······························

that his family has died in a house fire. Publishing the photograph may add to the man's suffering.

For the same reason, news companies are careful about naming victims of certain crimes, especially when the victims are children. The crimes are horrific enough. Mentioning names could make life more difficult for the victims.

In some situations news companies do show images of violence or human suffering. These images might prompt citizens or governments to take action. These situations can include natural disasters, outbreaks of disease or starvation in poor countries, or violent conflicts. Sometimes

"MINIMIZE HARM"

The Society of Professional Journalists' *Code of Ethics* reminds journalists to "Minimize Harm." In part the *Code of Ethics* says journalists should:

- *Show compassion for those who may be affected adversely by news coverage. Use special sensitivity when dealing with children and inexperienced sources or subjects.*

- *Be sensitive when seeking or using interviews or photographs of those affected by tragedy or grief.*
- *Be cautious about identifying juvenile suspects or victims of sex crimes.*
- *Be [careful] about naming criminal suspects before the formal filing of charges.*
- *Balance a criminal suspect's fair trial rights with the public's right to be informed.*

people don't know how bad the situation is until they see images of the sick, injured, or dead. Seeing those images might move people to donate money, volunteer, or urge their elected officials to take action.

One simple way to address this issue is to ask for the person's permission before taking a photograph or reporting sensitive information. This is not always possible. But sometimes it allows the journalist to tell an important story without causing pain to a person who is already suffering.

Admitting Mistakes

Regardless of how hard they try to be accurate, news companies do make mistakes. Common mistakes include misspelling a name, publishing the wrong photograph with a story, or typing the wrong number or date. Occasionally the mistake can be a big one, such as getting an important fact wrong.

Regardless of how hard they try to be accurate, news companies do make mistakes.

When a mistake is made, journalistic standards say the news company should publish a correction. A correction is a statement in which a news company admits the mistake and gives the correct

NBA FINALS GAME 6: MAVERICKS 105, HEAT 95
DALLAS WINS BEST-OF-7 SERIES 4-2

HEAT | POINT GUARD PROBLEMS

Heat just never got the point during Finals loss to more-organized Mavs

CONGRATULATIONS
MIAMI!

CELEBRATE THE 2011 NBA CHAMPIONS
WITH OFFICIAL MERCHANDISE FROM ADIDAS!
MEN'S LOCKER ROOM TEES AVAILABLE TODAY
WITH MORE STYLES FOR HIM, HER & KIDS ARRIVING DAILY

A Macy's advertisement in *The Miami Herald* congratulated the Miami Heat on winning the 2011 NBA Finals. The ad ran with the news story that the Dallas Mavericks clinched the title the night before. The *Herald* later published a correction.

information. Responsible news companies openly admit their mistakes so that it doesn't look as if they're trying to hide anything. This helps them keep their credibility with the public.

Changing Standards?

News companies in the United States have followed journalistic standards for many years. However, some people feel that news companies are forgetting the old rules of journalism.

In today's world news companies compete to be the first to break news. When a major event takes place, it may take time to weed out true information from rumors. In order to be the first to report a story, some news companies have reported unverified information.

For example, when Arizona congresswoman Gabrielle Giffords was shot at a public gathering in 2011, one news company reported that she had died. Other news companies repeated what the first news company had said, without verifying the facts.

When a major event takes place, it may take time to weed out true information from rumors.

Giffords' husband heard the news and believed his wife had died. In fact, she had not died but was seriously wounded and in the hospital. You can see how the rush to report the news can result

Reporting a news story before all facts have been checked can lead to false information. This was the case in the coverage of the shooting of Arizona congresswoman Gabrielle Giffords.

in some bad mistakes. These mistakes hurt news companies' credibility.

What do you think? Is it important for news companies to follow the journalistic standards, even if it takes longer to report a story? Is it ever OK to report a story immediately, before all of the facts have been checked?

CHAPTER 3

FAIRNESS AND BIAS

"Journalists must maintain an independence from those they cover."

—**Bill Kovach and Tom Rosenstiel,**
The Elements of Journalism

Journalists and news managers constantly make judgments about which news stories are important. They must also decide which pieces of information are essential to a story. These decisions affect what the public knows—or doesn't know—about news events.

Fairness is one of the most important values of American journalism.

Journalists have influence over what we know and think about the news. So they must be as fair as possible. In reporting, fairness means showing all sides of a story. It means that the reporter covering the story and the news company publishing the story are reporting all of the information that is available.

When a story is not fair, it is said to be slanted or biased.

Bias is the opposite of fairness. Bias means that a story is shown in a way that supports a particular opinion. A biased news story leaves out certain facts. It may try to persuade the audience to form a certain opinion.

In recent history the general public has grown to think of the mainstream media as less fair and more biased. One reason could be that the media actually have become more biased. Another possible reason is that people today are more aware of media bias than they were in the past. And yet another reason is that people may be confusing editorial opinion with news reporting. There are several different types of bias.

Advertiser Bias

Most media companies make money by selling advertisements. Without this money, they would go out of business. Advertiser bias occurs when a news company makes a reporting decision based on an advertiser's interests.

For example, imagine that a local hospital buys advertisements at a TV station. A reporter at the TV station learns that the hospital is under investigation for using dirty surgical tools. If the TV station reports this story, it will make the hospital look bad. Hospital managers may be upset with the TV station. They might pull their advertisements.

In a situation like this, most TV stations would report the story even though they might lose money as a result. However, if the TV station ignored the story in order to keep the advertiser happy, that would be an example of advertiser bias. It would not be bias if the TV station doesn't report the story because it lacks information. The advertiser's influence in the decision-making process is what makes it bias.

Corporate Bias

The media can also be biased toward their own business interests. Corporate bias occurs when

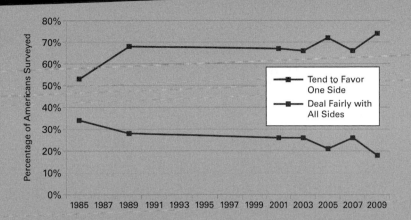

In a series of surveys between 1985 and 2009, Americans were asked whether the media deal fairly with all sides. From the start people believed that the media report the news in a one-sided manner. The belief grew as time went on.

Source: Pew Research Center for the People and the Press

a news company's reporting is influenced by the interests or policies of its corporate owner.

Many media companies are owned by large corporations. These corporations also own other types of businesses. For example, did you know that The Walt Disney Company owns the ABC television network, including ABC News? That means

The Walt Disney Company owns ABC News. If ABC News declined to report a story that made Disney look bad, that would be an example of corporate bias. . . . .

the same company that owns the Disney theme parks and movie studios also owns a news media company. ABC News reports on news involving Disney. Similarly, the NBC television network is partly owned by General Electric.

Usually companies are careful to keep their news reporting separate from their business interests. They make sure that their reporters are free to report on their own company, without being censored or punished. If somebody was hurt at a Disney theme park, ABC News would be expected to report the story.

Despite their efforts to show that they are free from corporate bias, large news companies are still accused of favoring their corporate owners from time to time.

In 2011 media giant Rupert Murdoch's British tabloid, *News of the World*, was accused of phone hacking and paying police sources for information. Many news organizations covered the story in depth. CNN and MSNBC spent approximately 16 minutes a night in prime-time coverage of the scandal. But Fox News, also owned by Murdoch, averaged less than three minutes of coverage a night. Many media outlets accused Fox News of intentionally giving little attention to a story that would reflect its owner in an unfavorable light.

Perceived Bias

Even if a news company is never influenced by its corporate owners, it still needs to worry about perceived bias. Perceived bias is when people believe that

> *Even if a news company is never influenced by its corporate owners, it still needs to worry about perceived bias.*

a news company is biased. Perceived bias can be just as damaging to a news company's credibility as actual bias.

One way news companies try to show the public that they are not biased is through disclosure statements. A disclosure statement appears in a news story. It tells the audience there is a relationship between the news company and the subject of the story. By openly admitting the connection, the news company shows that they are not trying to hide it. Still some people believe that if a media company is owned by a large corporation, it's almost impossible for them to avoid some corporate bias.

Political Bias

When people accuse the mass media of bias, they are often talking about political bias. Political bias occurs when reporting is influenced by a reporter's own political views, or by the political views of a media company.

Many reporters refuse to label themselves as Democrat or Republican. They don't publicly support candidates in political elections. Some of them don't even vote. They do this to show that they are fair and not biased.

However, most Americans believe that the media are politically biased. In a 2009 national survey, 78 percent of Republicans and 50 percent of Democrats said the media were politically biased. Sixty-two percent of Independents agreed with them.

In a 2009 national survey, 78 percent of Republicans and 50 percent of Democrats said the media were politically biased.

Does the media have a bias? When it comes to political bias, how do we tell the difference between perceived and real bias?

Bias can be hard to prove. A reporter will probably not admit to a bias when covering a story. In fact, the reporter might not even realize there was a bias. Most of the time, the audience forms their own opinions about whether reporting is biased. Here is an example:

In September 2004 the CBS News show *60 Minutes* reported a story about then-President George W. Bush's military record. The story said that when Bush was serving in the Texas Air National Guard in the 1970s, he ignored an order to appear for a physical examination. It also said that a friend of the Bush family tried to "sugar coat" an evaluation of his Guard service. Those claims were based on

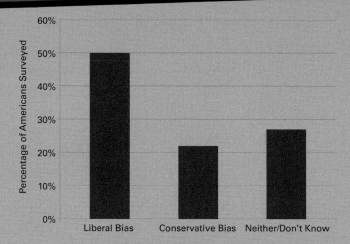

In a survey conducted in 2009, 50 percent of respondents said the media had a liberal bias. Twenty-two percent said the media had a conservative bias. Twenty-seven percent said the media were not biased, or that they were unaware of a bias in the media.

The terms "liberal" and "conservative" describe different viewpoints on public policy and social issues. Democrats tend to have liberal viewpoints. Republicans tend to have conservative viewpoints.

Source: Pew Research Center for the People and the Press

four documents allegedly written by a National Guard commander. The commander had died by the time the story was reported. At the time Bush, a Republican, was running for re-election against Senator John Kerry, a Democrat.

After the story was reported, questions were raised about whether the documents in the story were real. Eventually CBS admitted that they could not prove the documents were real. Four CBS news employees were fired as a result. CBS news anchor Dan Rather resigned from his position.

Later a survey found that 40 percent of the public believed CBS ran the story because "CBS News and Dan Rather are liberals who dislike President Bush." Only 10 percent of journalists agreed that bias was involved. Most journalists believed CBS ran the story before carefully checking facts because it was in a hurry to be the first to break the big story.

Racial Bias

Another type of media bias is racial bias. Racial bias occurs when the media are unfair in their coverage of a racial or ethnic group. This can mean that a news company unfairly focuses on negative stories involving certain races. It can also mean that the news company covers few positive stories about certain races. A news company might also fail to interview experts of various races for news stories.

One type of racial bias is known as "missing white woman syndrome." This is the claim that the mainstream media are more likely to report a story about a missing white woman than a missing woman of another race (or a man of any race).

For example, consider the cases of Laci Peterson and LaToyia Figueroa. Laci Peterson, a Caucasian woman, was pregnant when she disappeared from her home in Modesto, California, in 2002. The remains of Laci and her unborn child were found several months later. Her husband was eventually sentenced to death for the murders.

Additional media coverage might not have helped authorities find LaToyia Figueroa faster, but most people agree that her case should have received more attention. ·······································

Three years later LaToyia Figueroa, a woman of African-American and Hispanic descent, was pregnant when she vanished from her home in Philadelphia. The remains of LaToyia and her unborn child were found a month later. The father of the child was convicted on two counts of murder.

While the details of the two cases were similar, the Peterson case received constant coverage from the national media. The Figueroa case, however, received relatively little attention from national news outlets. At the time the national media was focused on the story of Natalee Holloway, a white teenager who had gone missing on the island of Aruba.

Many news managers believe that one way to reduce racial bias is to hire people of various races as news managers and reporters. They believe that if there are more diverse viewpoints in the newsroom, the reporting will also be more diverse. In 2009 non-whites made up around 13 percent of employees at U.S. newspapers—but 27.6 percent of the total U.S. population.

Other Types of Bias

There is a risk of bias whenever a reporter or news company has an opinion about the subject of a story. Here are just a few examples of controversial subjects where a reporter might be accused of slanting his or her reporting:

- Religion
- Science and evolution
- Global warming
- Homosexuality and gay marriage

BIAS AND CABLE NEWS

To understand how strongly a person's beliefs can influence his or her view of media bias, consider the cable news networks Fox News and CNN. Fox News, which promotes itself as "fair and balanced," is widely considered to have a conservative bias. CNN, meanwhile, is commonly believed to have a liberal bias.

In a survey conducted in 2009, 72 percent of conservatives had a positive view of Fox News. Only 44 percent had a positive view of CNN. On the other hand, 75 percent of liberals had a positive view of CNN. Only 43 percent had a positive view of Fox News. In other words, conservatives tend to think of Fox News as a good news source. Liberals tend to think of CNN as a good news source.

Can you imagine how both real and perceived bias might occur with these subjects? When thinking about bias, there are three points to remember.

First, most reporters and news companies try to be fair. They follow standards that require them to interview experts on all sides of a story. They have editors who double-check stories to make sure they are accurate and fair. When mistakes are made, the companies usually move quickly to show that they will not allow bias or the appearance of bias.

Second, most media bias is unintentional. Reporters sometimes give opinions without realizing it. Nobody decided that the disappearance of LaToyia Figueroa was unimportant, yet the national media focused on Natalee Holloway. Unintentional bias can be just as harmful as intentional bias.

Finally, people sometimes perceive bias where it does not exist. Some people have a hard time listening to viewpoints that differ from their own. For those people a fair story may seem slanted because it presents information they don't support.

What do you think? Does the media you follow have a slant? What might be your own bias? Is it always possible to keep bias out of the news?

CHAPTER 4

OTHER TYPES OF NEWS MEDIA

"In an era when the mainstream media has narrowed its lens, we're convinced readers yearn for the opposite ... We're also free to be an independent voice, devoid of the corporate allegiances and pressures that critics say too often skew today's media."

— *"About The Christian Science Monitor"* statement on the website of **The Christian Science Monitor**

When it comes to politics and other controversial issues, the mainstream media are supposed to be fair and not take sides. However, some people—both liberals and conservatives—believe the media are biased.

Other people find that the mainstream media do not cover the types of stories they're interested in. These people often turn to opinion journalism and alternative media for their news.

Opinion Journalism

Opinion journalism is a type of journalism that openly supports a point of view. Opinion journalists don't try to be fair. Instead they share their opinions about news events. They try to convince others to agree with them.

One type of opinion journalism is the opinion column—an essay in which the writer states a point of view on a subject. The writer explains why that point of view makes sense. Opinion columns appear in mainstream newspapers, magazines, and websites. The TV and radio version of an opinion column is often called commentary.

Opinion columns and commentary may include facts from news reports and quotes from experts, like a news story would. But opinion journalism is not expected to be balanced. The writer might pick facts and expert opinions that only support one side.

When you read a column or an editorial you get the opinion of the person writing it. You can decide whether you agree with the viewpoint. . . . .

Opinion columns and commentary also have persuasive language, which is not allowed in a news story. For example, an opinion column writer could say, "The death penalty should be outlawed." A reporter shouldn't say anything "should" or "should not" happen. A reporter is not supposed to give a point of view.

Another type of opinion journalism is the editorial, which is like an opinion column. However, an editorial is meant to give the point of view of the entire news company that is publishing it. Many newspapers declare their support for candidates for political offices in editorials.

Opinion columns and editorials are placed in a separate area of a newspaper, magazine, or website away from news stories. Columns that present a viewpoint are clearly labeled as opinion columns. On a radio or TV news show, an announcement is made before commentary is heard. This is to make sure nobody confuses opinion with news reporting.

However, people often decide that a media company is biased based on the opinion columns and editorials it publishes. If a newspaper often prints columns that support a liberal point of view, but rarely publishes columns with a conservative point of view, people might think that the entire newspaper has a liberal bias.

What do you think? If a news company publishes opinion columns and editorials that always favor one political side, does that mean the company's news reporting is biased?

Political Pundits and Cable News

Another type of opinion journalism is punditry. A pundit is a person who offers his or her opinion as an expert on politics, news events, or controversial issues. Pundits are sometimes called commentators. Many pundits actually are experts in the subjects they discuss. But some pundits get attention simply because they are loud and outrageous.

Pundits who have strong political viewpoints can be skilled at spin. It is a way of altering the truth to influence public opinion about an issue. Spin is a lot like bias, except that bias can be unintentional. Spin usually refers to the intentional distortion of information.

Many pundits have their own TV shows, radio shows, or websites. One of the most common places to find pundits is on cable news channels such as CNN, Fox News, and MSNBC. While these channels have news shows that report national and international events, they also have shows featuring political pundits. Often the pundits attract larger audiences than the news shows.

Some well-known pundits who have frequently appeared as guests on cable networks or have had their own shows include Bill O'Reilly, Glenn Beck, Keith Olbermann, and Rachel Maddow. If you watch one of these pundits, you will see that they are nothing like a TV news reporter. Most of the time is spent explaining why the pundit's opinion is right and everyone else is wrong. The appearances might include arguing, raised voices, and even name-calling. Politicians and political parties may be accused of lying to the public or working

"DEATH PANELS" AND SPIN

In 2009 conservative pundit and former vice presidential candidate Sarah Palin wrote on her Facebook page that President Barack Obama's health care plan for the nation would set up "death panels." She said these panels would decide which members of society were worthy of receiving health care. In the following weeks, the phrase "death panels" was repeated numerous times by other conservative pundits and politicians. They warned that the elderly would be at risk of losing their health care. In two polls conducted within weeks of Palin's original statement, approximately 30 percent of the people surveyed thought that Obama's health care plan would allow the government to make decisions about when to stop providing medical care to the elderly.

In reality Obama's plan simply provided government funding to pay for doctor visits in which patients could discuss end-of-life issues. Whether this was a good idea, it was a far cry from death panels. This is an example of using spin tactics and lies to influence public opinion on an issue.

against America's interests. Not all pundits behave this way, but many of them do. Many people feel that these types of shows are not journalism at all, but entertainment.

Blogs and Aggregators

Many pundits also have websites called blogs. A blogger can easily publish information, opinions, and links to other websites. It's not just pundits and reporters who have blogs. Many people who have strong opinions about politics or social issues have their own blogs. A person does not need to have any journalism training or experience to write a blog.

A type of website similar to a blog is an aggregator. A news aggregator is a website that is made up of links to news stories on other websites. One of the first news aggregators was the Drudge Report, launched in 1996 by Matt Drudge. The conservative Drudge Report offers a collection of links to various news stories on mainstream media websites as well as alternative and international media websites. The editors of the Drudge Report and other aggregators decide which news stories to link, based on what they believe is interesting or important.

Conservative political pundit Glenn Beck began his career by hosting a radio show before starting his own TV show for Fox News in 2008. Beck left Fox in 2011 and started GBTV, an Internet streaming video network. ·····················

Some people like to get their news from blogs and aggregators because they agree with the viewpoints of the people who run them. If a person has a conservative political viewpoint, he or she might prefer the opinions and news links selected by a blogger or aggregator who supports those views. An important thing about pundits, blogs, and aggregators is that they usually comment on news

Occasionally a blogger or aggregator may be the first to break a news story.

that has already been reported by the media. Occasionally a blogger or aggregator may be the first to break a news story. However, it is rare for these people to travel to the location of a news event and report the news firsthand.

Alternative and Independent Media

Alternative media are in a separate category from opinion journalism. They are news companies that provide an "alternative" to mainstream media. Alternative media may cover different stories than the mainstream media. They may cover the same stories in a different way.

Many people who use alternative media believe that the mainstream media are deeply influenced by corporate bias. They believe the corporations are more interested in making money than informing the public. As a result these people think that the mainstream media spend too much time on entertainment news and ignore more important stories.

Alternative media are not owned by large corporations. Instead they are usually owned

At the 2008 Democratic National Convention, a lounge was set up for bloggers to use. Blogging has become a popular way for citizens to report news and give their opinions on it.

by smaller companies or nonprofit companies. Nonprofits use the money they earn to pay for reporting, instead of generating profits for investors or corporate owners. Alternative media are often called independent media. Many alternative media companies have advertisers, but they also ask for donations from the public.

Examples of alternative media that cover national and international news include the newspaper *The Christian Science Monitor* and the magazine *Mother Jones*. These publications also have websites. There are also alternative news companies in cities and towns all over the United States.

The Internet has also made it possible for people to follow news coverage from other countries.

SCHOOL-SPONSORED MEDIA

School newspapers, TV stations, and websites can be described as alternative media. They often report different stories than the mainstream media, or report stories from a different angle.

However, school-run media may not be as independent as other media when it comes to freedom from censorship. Newspapers and other student media funded by public universities are the most free. They have similar rights in most states as a corporate-owned or nonprofit news company. Student media at public schools for students in kindergarten through high school have somewhat less freedom. The United States Supreme Court has ruled that school officials may censor them under certain circumstances. Student media at private schools and colleges have the least protection from censorship. Those newspapers are owned by private companies and are not protected by the First Amendment.

Many Americans look at the website of the Arabic TV channel, Al Jazeera. When news happens in the Middle East, Al Jazeera may offer different information and perspectives than the mainstream American media.

Alternative news companies have one thing in common with mainstream media: They hire professional journalists who travel to the locations of news events and report information firsthand. This is different from opinion journalists and pundits, who comment on already reported news.

Even though they are usually free of corporate bias, other types of bias can still influence alternative media. Many alternative news companies are believed to represent certain political points of view. For example, the magazine *Mother Jones* is considered a liberal publication. Just as people make mainstream media choices based on their own political opinions, they may also seek out alternative media sources that support their personal views.

What do you think? Would you seek out news sources that support your personal views? What is the disadvantage of only using news sources that represent a single point of view?

CHAPTER 5

CITIZEN JOURNALISM

"There's a plane in the Hudson. I'm on the ferry going to pick up the people. Crazy."

—Twitter post of Janis Krums, who published the first photo of an airplane that had landed in the Hudson River in 2009

There was a time, not long ago, when average citizens did not have much involvement with news coverage. A person could alert the media to a news story by calling or writing to a news company with a news tip. Many reporters over the years have broken stories as a result of information from citizens who saw news.

In the past a person could contact a news company after a story had been printed in the newspaper or broadcast on TV. The person might have found a mistake or have more information about the news event that the reporter didn't know about. But by that time, the story had already been made public.

Today, thanks to the Internet and smartphones, average citizens can help reporters do a better job of covering the news. Citizen journalism is what happens when members of the public report the news. It may also be called participatory journalism.

The most common way for a person to participate in citizen journalism is to provide information, pictures, or video about a breaking news event. Here are some examples:

- On January 15, 2009, a US Airways airplane made an emergency landing in the Hudson River in New York City. Before any news media could arrive at the scene, a person on a ferry took a photo of the partially submerged airplane with his cell phone. He posted the photo to his Twitter account. That photo immediately appeared on

A citizen journalist used his smartphone to photograph protests in Bangkok, Thailand, in December 2010. Citizen journalists can provide the public with images and information from the scene of an event.

blogs and news websites as the first image from the scene.

- During political protests in Iran in the summer of 2009, the Iranian government took extreme measures to block reporters from showing the world what was happening. During that time private citizens secretly took photos and made videos of the violence in the streets and managed to publish them online for the world to view. With professional reporters banned from the scene, citizen journalists became a key source of information and images.

- A devastating earthquake and tsunami hit Japan in the spring of 2011, killing thousands. Soon after citizen photos and videos of the disaster and damage appeared all over the Internet.

Ordinary citizens can do a lot to help the media report the news. Now that many people have smartphones with cameras and Internet access, they can be the first "eyes and ears" at the scene.

Ordinary citizens can do a lot to help the media report the news.

Risks of Citizen Journalism

Although citizen journalism can be helpful, news companies must be careful when they publish material provided by the public. This is because news companies usually can't verify the truth of the information they receive from the public. There are dishonest people who might alter a photograph or lie about the time and place a video was taken.

A basic rule of journalism is that a reporter must confirm the truth of information before it is published. If a news company publishes something that turns out to be fake, the company's credibility may be seriously damaged. On the other hand,

THE DANGERS OF CITIZEN JOURNALISM

Reporters working in areas where violent conflicts are taking place may risk their lives to get news. Since citizen journalists often take over the job of gathering information when officials have banned reporters from an area, they too often face risks. In fact, the risks may be heightened, since the government has banned reporters from the area. These governments may punish people for taking photographs or videos when reporters have been banned.

if a news company decides not to publish any information or photos provided by the public, then their audience would miss out on a lot of information.

Some news companies have found a compromise: They publish information provided by the public in a separate area of their websites. The website clearly identifies the information and images as material provided by citizens.

However, problems still occur. In 2008 a person posted information in the citizen journalism section of the CNN website claiming that the founder of Apple computers, Steve Jobs, had been rushed to the hospital with a heart attack. The rumor was false. Apple's company stock price immediately dropped, even though CNN.com quickly removed the post.

Citizen journalism can have a valuable role in reporting news events. However, it's important to remember that information provided by the public may not be as reliable as information from mainstream news organizations.

Do you think citizen journalism is helpful? Why or why not? Would you rely on this type of news as your sole news source?

In a free society, not only professionals report the news. . . . .

CHAPTER 6

BE A SMART NEWS CONSUMER

"I think the one lesson I have learned is that there is no substitute for paying attention."

—Diane Sawyer, ABC evening news anchor

Most reporters and news companies work hard to report the news in a way that is correct and complete. Many of them believe strongly in the media's responsibility to inform citizens of events that may shape their lives. However, the media are not perfect. From time to time, the media may be influenced by advertisers, business interests, or political beliefs.

The media also make mistakes, no matter how hard they try to avoid them. The media may overlook important stories because they are not paying close enough attention to certain groups of people or parts of the world.

For these reasons and more, it is important for you to know how the media work. You should not blindly

accept everything you see or hear in a news report. Here are some things you can do to be a smart news consumer:

Use Multiple News Sources

Just as journalists check with at least two reliable sources before reporting information, a smart news consumer uses multiple news sources. This is especially important during breaking news events. Many news companies make mistakes while covering breaking news, when everyone is rushing to report the story. By looking at multiple sources, you might discover that some have more accurate information than others.

Using multiple news sources will also provide you with a more complete view of the news. While most companies cover the same big stories, there are

There are many news sources available on the Internet. To make sure you are getting factual, unbiased news, you should consult several sources.

many other stories that some news sources cover and others ignore.

Pay Attention to Bylines and Photo Credits

With stories and photos in print newspapers and on the Web, look for bylines and photo credits. They show who reported a story or took a photograph. They also note whether the reporter or photographer works for the news company that's publishing the information or for a wire service. Wire services are news companies that provide stories, photos, and video for other news companies. The Associated Press is one such wire service.

It's common for mass media to use wire services to follow stories they can't cover themselves. For example, a newspaper in Wisconsin may not be able to send reporters to Louisiana to cover a story about an oil spill in the Gulf of Mexico. Instead that newspaper—along with many other news companies—would print a version of the story and perhaps a photograph provided by The Associated Press. This explains why media outlets around the country often have identical news stories. If a news company is using a story provided by The Associated Press or another outside source, it is supposed to mention that in the byline.

Ask Questions about the Reporting

Now that you understand the standards of good journalism, you can check to see whether news stories follow those rules. For example, are the sources of information clearly identified? Has the reporter attempted to interview sources on all sides of a story? Does the reporter's company have any connection to the story? If so, has the reporter included a disclaimer statement? If the answer to any of these questions is no, you should definitely check other news sources to find a more reliable version of the story.

Separate Fact from Opinion

Does the person reporting the story appear to have a point of view about the story? It's not unusual for a reporter to appear sad when reporting a tragedy such as an earthquake. Nearly everyone agrees that death and destruction are terrible things. However, if the story is about a controversial subject such as politics or religion, a fair reporter should not appear to support one side of the story over the other. A fair reporter would quote people on both sides of the controversy but would not suggest that one side is right and the other side is wrong.

Beware of Advertorials

An advertorial is a kind of advertisement that is made to look like a news story. Advertorials are used by companies that want to market their products, or political interest groups that want to promote their beliefs. Advertorials can be an effective type of advertising because they look like news stories. They sometimes trick people into believing they are real news.

Advertorials might appear in newspapers, magazines, and websites next to real news stories. They might be written in the style of a news story, with real-looking headlines and quotes from

A reporter should not appear to support one side of a story over another. ·

sources. On TV advertorials could be long shows or short commercials that look a lot like real news reports.

If you look closely, you will see that advertorials are nearly always labeled as advertising. There will be a small bit of text next to the advertorial in a newspaper, or on the TV screen, noting the information is a paid advertisement. However, you can mistakenly overlook that label and be tricked into thinking you are viewing news.

Special Rules for Online News

The Internet makes it possible to access news from all over the world at the touch of a button. However, you need to be careful when checking news online. When a story is online, it's easy to get confused about when a story was published or whether you're looking at the complete version of the story.

First check the date stamp of an online news story. The date stamp is the information at the top of a news story that tells you when the story was published or updated. Oftentimes the date stamp may inform you of the specific time of day the story was published or updated. It's important to check the date stamp, since there are often many versions of online news stories. If you are not careful, you may be looking at an old version of a news story that is now out-of-date.

> **The Internet makes it possible to access news from all over the world at the touch of a button.**

Pay attention to whether you are looking at a real news website, or a website that is simply republishing news reported by other media companies. For example, if you are looking at a blog or another website that claims an issue was reported in *The New York Times*, it's best to find that story on *The New York Times'* website. Read the complete story to make sure you understand the whole story and not just part of it.

In a country with a free press, the media and the public all have responsibilities to uphold. The media are responsible for covering news events in a fair and complete manner. This will help citizens make informed decisions during political elections and in their daily lives. Meanwhile, the public has a responsibility to stay informed and to demand that the media continue to practice the standards of good journalism. Are you prepared to be a smart news consumer?

PUBLIC PERCEPTIONS OF MEDIA ACCURACY

In a public survey conducted in 2009, only 29 percent of Americans believed that the media usually get the facts straight. Approximately two-thirds of Americans said news stories are often inaccurate. For many years the public's view of media accuracy has been declining. What do you think? Can you trust the media's news?

MEDIA LITERACY 101

Here are some exercises that will help you experience media literacy concepts first-hand.

1 Using a printed newspaper or news magazine, try to find the following:

At least one example of an editorial or opinion column.

> On the page is there a label that identifies it as an editorial or opinion column?

> Are there any clues that you're looking at an opinion and not a balanced news story?

At least one example of an advertorial.

> How does the newspaper or magazine help you tell the difference between advertorials and actual news stories?

> Do you think this difference would be clear to the average reader, or could people be confused and think they're reading news instead of an ad?

2 Using a printed copy of a newspaper, count the number of stories on the first two pages.

> How many of these stories are hard news?

> How many of these stories are entertainment news?

> Which story is most interesting to you, and why?

> Now identify the lead story.

> Do you agree that the lead story is the most important story in the newspaper? Why or why not? Are there any other stories that could be the lead story?

3 Using a printed newspaper or a news website, look at the byline of at least 20 different news stories.

Out of the 20 stories, how many of them have bylines that mention The Associated Press or another wire service?

Does the news company make it easy to tell which stories were written by reporters who work for that news company?

Now imagine that all of the newspapers and TV and radio stations in your city obtain their news from the same wire service. Can you think of any resulting problems?

4 Pick a popular national or international news story. Read a printed newspaper article, watch a TV news report, read an online news article, and listen to a radio broadcast about the same story.

Did the news gathered from these media sources have any similarities? Any differences?

Were your feelings and opinions influenced by the way you received the news? How so?

NEWS

GLOSSARY

advertorial
advertisement made to look like a news story

bias
something that supports a particular opinion or viewpoint

blog
online journal, short for weblog

censorship
limiting what can be said, written, or taught

commentary
TV or radio segment in which the speaker states a point of view on a subject

credibility
public trust in a news company to report the news accurately and fairly

defamation
distribution of false information that damages an individual's good reputation

disclosure statement
a written or spoken note that informs an audience of a relationship between the news company reporting a story and the story's subject

editorial
an article that represents the point of view of the news company publishing it

fairness
covering all angles of a story and presenting relevant and available information

news aggregator
website that consists of links to news stories on other websites

news tip
information about an event that has happened or is about to happen

opinion column
a written column that states the writer's point of view on a subject

opinion journalism
a type of news media that openly supports a point of view

perceive
to become aware of something

verification
confirming facts by witnessing them directly, or checking with at least two trustworthy sources

ADDITIONAL RESOURCES

Investigate Further

Botzakis, Stergios. *What's Your Source?: Questioning the News.* Mankato, Minn.: Capstone Press, 2009.

DiConsiglio, John. *The News Never Stops.* Chicago: Raintree, 2011.

Marcovitz, Hal. *Bias in the Media.* Detroit: Lucent Books, 2010.

Streissguth, Thomas. *Media Bias.* New York: Marshall Cavendish Benchmark, 2007.

Internet Sites

Use FactHound to find Internet sites related to this book. All of the sites on FactHound have been researched by our staff.

Here's all you do:

Visit *www.facthound.com*

Type in this code: 9780756545178

Keep Exploring Media Literacy!

Read the other books in this series:

The Big Push: *How Popular Culture Is Always Selling*
Selling Ourselves: *Marketing Body Images*
Violence as Entertainment: *Why Aggression Sells*

SOURCE NOTES

Chapter 1

Page 4, opening quote: Bill Kovach and Tom Rosenstiel. *The Elements of Journalism: What Newspeople Should Know and the Public Should Expect.* New York: Three Rivers Press, 2007, p. 10.

Page 6, graph: "Americans Spending More Time Following the News." The Pew Research Center for the People and the Press. 12 Sept. 2010. 22 July 2011. http://people-press.org/files/legacy-pdf/652.pdf

Page 18, graph: "Haiti Remains Public's Main Concern." The Pew Research Center for the People and the Press. 3 Feb. 2010. 20 May 2011. http://pewresearch.org/pubs/1485/public-focus-haiti-state-of-the-union

Page 18, line 3: Ibid.

Chapter 2

Page 20, opening quote: Deborah Halpern Wenger. *Advancing the Story: Broadcast Journalism in a Multimedia World.* Washington, D.C.: CQ Press, 2011, p. 51.

Page 21, line 6: United States. Bill of Rights. The Charters of Freedom. Bill of Rights Transcript. 20 May 2011. www.archives.gov/exhibits/charters/bill_of_rights_transcript.html

Page 29, sidebar, line 7: "SPJ Code of Ethics." Society of Professional Journalists. 22 May 2011. www.spj.org/pdf/ethicscode.pdf

Chapter 3

Page 34, opening quote: *The Elements of Journalism: What Newspeople Should Know and the Public Should Expect,* p. 118.

Page 37, graph: "Press Accuracy Rating Hits Two Decade Low." The Pew Research Center for the People and the Press. 13 Sept. 2009. 20 May 2011. http://people-press.org/2009/09/13/press-accuracy-rating-hits-two-decade-low

Page 41, line 3: Ibid.

Page 42, graph: Ibid.

Page 43, line 7: "People and Press Differ About Partisan Bias, Accuracy and Press Freedom, New Annenberg Public Policy Center Survey Shows." The Annenberg Public Policy Center. 24 May 2005. 20 May 2011. www.annenbergpublicpolicycenter.org/Downloads/IoD_Survey_Findings_Summer2005/Partisan_Bias_20050524.pdf

Page 43, line 23: "Race Bias in Media Coverage of Missing Women?" CNN.com. 17 March 2007. 20 May 2011. http://transcripts.cnn.com/TRANSCRIPTS/0603/17/sbt.01.html

Page 46, sidebar, line 12: "Press Accuracy Rating Hits Two Decade Low."

Chapter 4

Page 48, opening quote: "About The Christian Science Monitor." *The Christian Science Monitor*. 20 May 2011. www.csmonitor.com/About/The-Monitor-difference

Page 53, sidebar, line 19: Angie Drobnic Holan. "PolitiFact's Lie of the Year: 'Death panels.'" PolitiFact.com. 18 Dec. 2009. 20 May 2011. www.politifact.com/truth-o-meter/article/2009/dec/18/politifact-lie-year-death-panels

Chapter 5

Page 60, opening quote: Janis Krums. Twitter. 15 Jan. 2009. 20 May 2011. http://twitter.com/#!/jkrums/status/1121915133

Chapter 6

Page 66, opening quote: Ted Goodman, ed. *The Forbes Book of Business Quotations: 10,000 Thoughts on the Business of Life*. New York: Black Dog and Leventhal Publishers, 2006, p. 393.

Page 73, sidebar, line 1: "Press Accuracy Rating Hits Two Decade Low."

SELECT BIBLIOGRAPHY

Freedom Forum First Amendment Center. 20 May 2011. www.freedomforum.org

Kovach, Bill, and Tom Rosenstiel. *The Elements of Journalism: What Newspeople Should Know and the Public Should Expect*. New York: Three Rivers Press, 2007.

The Pew Research Center for the People and the Press. 18 July 2011. http://people-press.org

Reporters Without Borders for Press Freedom. 21 July 2011. http://en.rsf.org

Vaughn, Stephen L. *Encyclopedia of American Journalism*. New York: Routledge, 2008.

Wenger, Deborah Halpern. *Advancing the Story: Broadcast Journalism in a Multimedia World*. Washington, D.C.: CQ Press, 2011.

INDEX

ABOUT THE AUTHOR

Barb Palser is director of digital media at McGraw-Hill Broadcasting Company, where she oversees four local TV station websites. She is also a regular columnist and feature writer for *American Journalism Review*, a magazine for journalists and journalism students.

C.Lit PN 4731 .P245 2012
Palser, Barb.
Choosing news